FREEDOM'S PROMISE

FANNIE LOU HAMER
CIVIL RIGHTS ACTIVIST

BY DUCHESS HARRIS, JD, PHD

WITH MARNE VENTURA

Core Library

An Imprint of Abdo Publishing
abdobooks.com

Cover image: Fannie Lou Hamer was an African American civil rights activist in the 1960s and 1970s.

abdocorelibrary.com

Published by Abdo Publishing, a division of ABDO, PO Box 398166, Minneapolis, Minnesota 55439. Copyright © 2020 by Abdo Consulting Group, Inc. International copyrights reserved in all countries. No part of this book may be reproduced in any form without written permission from the publisher. Core Library™ is a trademark and logo of Abdo Publishing.

Printed in the United States of America, North Mankato, Minnesota
032019
092019

Cover Photo: Warren K Leffler/PhotoQuest/Archive Photos/Getty Images
Interior Photos: Warren K Leffler/PhotoQuest/Archive Photos/Getty Images, 1; William J. Smith/AP Images, 5; Everett Collection/Newscom, 6–7; Bill Hudson/AP Images, 11, 22–23; Red Line Editorial, 12, 30; AP Images, 14–15; Everett Collection/Newscom, 17; Bob Child/AP Images, 18; Dick Strobel/AP Images, 28–29, 43; Bettmann/Getty Images, 33, 39; Rogelio V. Solis/AP Images, 36–37

Editor: Maddie Spalding
Series Designer: Claire Vanden Branden

Library of Congress Control Number: 2018966001

Publisher's Cataloging-in-Publication Data

Names: Harris, Duchess, author | Ventura, Marne, author.
Title: Fannie Lou Hamer: civil rights activist / by Duchess Harris and Marne Ventura
Other title: Civil rights activist
Description: Minneapolis, Minnesota: Abdo Publishing, 2020 | Series: Freedom's promise | Includes online resources and index.
Identifiers: ISBN 9781532118722 (lib. bdg.) | ISBN 9781532172908 (ebook)
Subjects: LCSH: Hamer, Fannie Lou--Juvenile literature. | African American women civil rights workers--Biography--Juvenile literature. | Minorities--Suffrage--United States--Juvenile literature. | Mississippi Freedom Democratic Party--Juvenile literature.
Classification: DDC 973.049607 [B]--dc23

CONTENTS

A LETTER FROM DUCHESS 4

CHAPTER ONE
The Right to Vote 6

CHAPTER TWO
Early Life and Activism 14

CHAPTER THREE
This Bus Is Too Yellow 22

CHAPTER FOUR
Hamer Speaks Up 28

CHAPTER FIVE
Hamer's Legacy 36

Fast Facts 42

Stop and Think 44

Glossary 45

Online Resources 46

Learn More 46

About the Authors 47

Index 48

A LETTER FROM DUCHESS

In 1964 African American civil rights activist Fannie Lou Hamer gave a speech at the Democratic National Convention. She described the discrimination and violence she and other Black people faced. She was forced to take a difficult literacy test when she tried to register to vote in 1962. These tests were designed to keep Black people from voting. In her speech, Hamer also described being unjustly arrested and beaten in jail. Her experiences were common among Black people in the South at the time. Hamer wanted to make the public more aware of these injustices.

Hamer's 1964 speech was broadcast on major news networks throughout the country. Her words influenced others to take action. In 1965 President Lyndon B. Johnson signed the Voting Rights Act. This act banned obstacles that kept Black people from voting.

This book explores Hamer's life and legacy. Join me in learning about this influential civil rights leader. Follow me on a journey that tells the story of the promise of freedom.

Fannie Lou Hamer gave many speeches in support of African Americans' civil rights.

DO YOU WANT
REGISTER
THIS DATE
APRIL
CO-SPONSORED BY AL

THE RIGHT TO VOTE

On August 31, 1962, Fannie Lou Hamer waited outside a courthouse in Indianola, Mississippi. Hamer was a 45-year-old black farmworker. She stood with 17 of her neighbors and coworkers. They were all African Americans. They had traveled to the courthouse by bus that morning. They were there to register to vote.

The white clerk only let two people into the courthouse. One of them was Hamer. The clerk told Hamer that she would have to pass a literacy test. If she did not pass the test, she would not be allowed to register to vote.

In the mid-1900s, many African Americans were eager to register to vote and have their voices heard.

Hamer knew that the US Constitution gave her the right to vote. She had learned this earlier at a political meeting. But no one had told her that she would have to pass a test.

Some of the questions on the test were about the state constitution. They were confusing. Hamer had never studied the state constitution. She and her friend both failed the test. Still, Hamer did not give up. As a citizen of the United States, she wanted to have a say in how the country was run. She told the courthouse clerk that she would be back. She was determined to register to vote.

VOTING OBSTACLES

The Fifteenth Amendment gave black men the right to vote in 1870. The Nineteenth Amendment was later passed in 1920. It gave all American women the right to vote. But southern states came up with ways to stop black men and women from voting. They charged poll taxes. They created difficult literacy tests. Black people who did not pay these taxes or pass these tests were not allowed to vote.

THE FIGHT FOR CIVIL RIGHTS

Hamer's experience at the courthouse was not unusual for African Americans in the South at the time. After the American Civil War (1861–1865), slavery was abolished in the United States. Black people who had been enslaved were freed. But many still worked on the same plantations where they had been enslaved. They were not paid fairly. They lived in poverty. They faced discrimination in other ways too. Jim Crow laws in the South enforced racial segregation. Racial segregation was the forced separation of white and black people. Black people had to use separate services and facilities, such as schools and restrooms. They did not have the same opportunities as white people.

In the 1960s, some African Americans could not read or write. This was a legacy left behind by slavery. It had been illegal to teach enslaved people to read or write. After slavery ended, it was still difficult for black people to get a good education. Unlike many of her coworkers, Hamer could read and write. But the literacy test was not a simple measure of her reading and writing abilities. White officials made the test difficult and unfair for black people. They asked questions that most people would not be able to answer. They gave literacy tests to white people too. But they usually gave white people much easier questions. In that way, they controlled who passed the tests.

In February 1965, a group of black youths protested voting segregation in Selma, Alabama.

ONE MAN ONE VOTE
OPEN THE
WE WILL OVERCOME
LET OUR PARENTS REGISTER
OPEN THE REGISTRA OFFIC
WHAT IN THE "L" ARE YOU STANDING FOR
LET OUR PARENTS VOTE
LET OUR PEOPLE VOTE
WE NEED FREE ELECTIONS
C. Clark
Monday Feb. 1,

BLACK VOTER REGISTRATION IN THE SOUTH

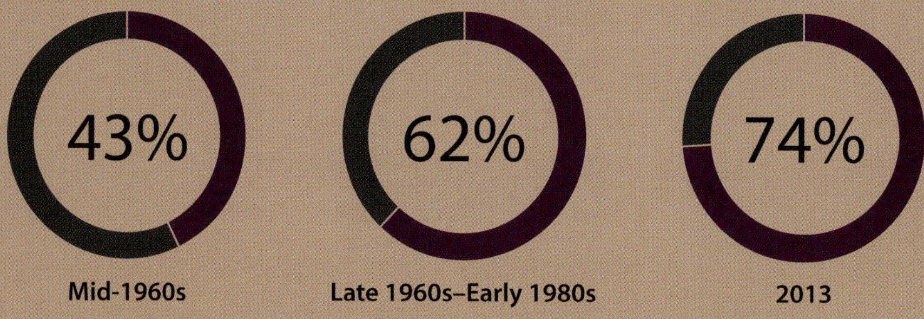

The above charts show how the percentage of African Americans who registered to vote in the South has changed over time. What trend do you notice? What may be some reasons for this trend?

Hamer's trip to the courthouse inspired her to fight for change. She decided she would do whatever she could to gain equal rights for herself and for other African Americans. She began by organizing a group to help black people register to vote in Mississippi.

In the years that followed, Hamer continued to fight for African Americans' political rights. Many white people opposed and targeted her. But she never let fear stop her from speaking out to make life better for African Americans.

STRAIGHT TO THE SOURCE

Bennie G. Thompson is a black representative from Mississippi. He gave a speech about Hamer in 2017:

Tonight, I recognize a civil rights hero whose work is no small part of the reason I and many other African American members of Congress are able to stand before you today. Ms. Hamer taught black Mississippians how to read and write in order for them to pass discriminatory voter tests designed to prevent black Americans from utilizing their right to vote.

I am happy to report to you now the sheriff, the chancery clerk, the circuit clerk and four of the five county supervisors are African Americans. So Mrs. Hamer's work has not been in vain.

Source: DeNeen L. Brown. "Civil Rights Crusader Fannie Lou Hamer Defied Men—and Presidents—Who Tried to Silence Her." *Washington Post.* Washington Post, October 6, 2017. Web. Accessed November 8, 2018.

Back It Up

The author of this passage is using evidence to support a point. Write a paragraph describing the point the author is making. Then write down two or three pieces of evidence the author uses to make the point.

EARLY LIFE AND ACTIVISM

Fannie Lou Hamer was born on October 6, 1917, in Montgomery County, Mississippi. She was the youngest of 20 children. Her parents were sharecroppers. Sharecroppers rented land that they farmed. They gave the land owners some of their crops at each harvest. Fannie Lou and her family lived and worked on a cotton plantation. They were paid very little. They often could not afford enough food. They lived in a tiny shack.

When Fannie Lou was six years old, she too went to work picking cotton. She was only able to go to school for a few months

In the early 1900s, many black people were forced to work as sharecroppers in the South.

After the Civil War, many former slaves worked on plantations in the South as sharecroppers. They lived in houses that belonged to white plantation owners. They grew crops on a plot of the plantation owner's land. They had to buy seeds, tools, clothing, and food on credit from the plantation owner's store. Often the prices at the store were unfairly high. At harvest time, the plantation owners sold the crops and used the profits to pay themselves back for the sharecroppers' rent, food, and supplies. Then they paid a portion of the remaining money to the sharecroppers. Often not much money was left over.

each year. When she was 12 years old, she dropped out of school to work full time on the plantation. She did not have a choice. Her family needed her help.

Fannie Lou once told her mother that she wished she could be white. Then, she believed, she would have all the clothes and food she needed. She would not have to work all the time. She would not be poor. Her mother told her that she should be proud to be black.

Civil rights activists sang songs to help each other through difficult times in the 1960s.

Fannie Lou learned many songs from her mother.

She sang to ease the pain and hardship of everyday life.

Fannie Lou would later use songs to help other people

through hard times.

Sharecroppers usually lived in small houses on plantations.

A GROWING FAMILY

In 1944 Fannie Lou married Perry "Pap" Hamer. Fannie Lou and Pap moved to a plantation outside of Ruleville, Mississippi. They worked as sharecroppers. When the plantation owner discovered that Fannie Lou could read and write, he asked her to be his timekeeper. In this job, she kept track of the time that sharecroppers worked. In addition to farming and timekeeping, Fannie Lou was paid to clean the plantation owner's house.

Fannie Lou loved children. She hoped to have a big family. She and Pap tried unsuccessfully to have a baby. They adopted two girls. One girl's mother was not able to take care of her. The other child had been injured when a tub of hot water was accidentally spilled on her. The girl's family was very poor, and they had many children. They were not able to care for her, so the Hamers offered to help.

In 1961 Fannie Lou went to the hospital to have a growth called a tumor removed. But the doctor did more than just remove her tumor. He performed another surgery on her without her permission. This surgery was called sterilization. It made her unable to have children. Many white doctors at the time performed forced sterilizations on women of color and women they didn't think would be good mothers. By the 1960s, doctors had sterilized thousands of women.

Fannie Lou later learned what had happened to her. She was angry and heartbroken. This injustice helped motivate her to fight for African Americans' civil rights.

A CIVIL RIGHTS MEETING

In the summer of 1962, Fannie Lou went to a meeting of the Student Nonviolent Coordinating Committee (SNCC). SNCC (pronounced "snick") was a civil rights group. Its goal was to help black people achieve equal rights. At the meeting, one of the group's leaders talked about the importance of voting. He explained that voters had elected many of the officials who treated black people unfairly. If many black people voted, they could help elect fairer officials. Fannie Lou understood the importance of voting. She wanted to have a say in how her community was run. She decided to join a group of SNCC volunteers that was going to register to vote.

FURTHER EVIDENCE

Chapter Two covers Fannie Lou's early life. What was one of the main points of this chapter? What evidence is included to support this point? Read the article at the website below. Does the information on the website support the main point of the chapter? Does it present new evidence?

FANNIE LOU HAMER: CIVIL RIGHTS ACTIVIST
abdocorelibrary.com/fannie-lou-hamer

6TH AVE

THIS BUS IS TOO YELLOW

I n August 1962, Fannie Lou hoped to become a voter at the Indianola courthouse. She filled out a long form. On the form, she was asked to write her address and her employer's name. She also had to say that she had never committed a crime.

After filling out the form, Fannie Lou had to take a literacy test. She did not pass the test. She got back on the bus to go home. The bus driver headed to Ruleville. On the way, a police officer made the bus pull over. The driver was African American. The police officer arrested the driver. When the passengers

In the 1960s, police often used force and violence against African American protesters.

asked why, the police officer said that the bus was too yellow. This was not actually a crime. The police officer made up this charge in order to arrest the driver.

Fannie Lou could see that her friends were scared. The officer could arrest them all. To calm them down, Fannie Lou started to sing. It worked. Her friends listened or sang along. It took their minds off their fears.

The officer told the driver he would have to pay a fine in order to be released. The driver did not have enough money, so the passengers pitched in. When the fine was paid, the officer let the driver go. Fannie Lou and the others made it home to Ruleville.

BAD NEWS

The clerks in the Indianola courthouse told Fannie Lou's boss that she tried to register to vote. Her boss, the plantation owner, was angry. He did not think black people should have the right to vote. He told Fannie Lou that if she did not give up on trying to vote, she would have to leave the plantation. Fannie Lou told him that she would not give up.

Fannie Lou had worked on the plantation for 18 years. Now the plantation owner told her that she was fired. He told her to get out of the house. But the Hamers still owed the plantation owner money. He had loaned them money for the house, seeds, tools, and food. Pap had to stay and work until the debt was paid. Fannie Lou took her two daughters and went to stay with friends in Ruleville.

A few weeks after Fannie Lou's move, white men fired 16 shots into the house where she and her daughters were staying. Luckily, no one was hurt. This type of attack was common in the South at the time. White people committed violence to threaten and intimidate black people.

THE MISSISSIPPI DELTA

The Hamers lived and worked in the Mississippi Delta. This region is located between the Yazoo and Mississippi rivers. The soil in the delta is rich and good for growing crops. Before the Civil War, many people built farms and enslaved people in the area. After the war, the sharecropping system kept black farmworkers in poverty. Today, the delta is still the poorest region of Mississippi. Mississippi is the poorest US state.

FANNIE LOU FIGHTS BACK

SNCC leaders noticed that Fannie Lou was good at convincing other people to join the cause. They asked her to work as a field organizer for SNCC. In this job, she visited people in her community.

She encouraged them to learn about their rights and register to vote.

When Pap left the plantation to join Fannie Lou, the plantation owner kept Pap's car. The plantation owner also kept everything in the house. Pap was left with nothing. The Hamers had to live on the ten dollars per week that SNCC paid Fannie Lou. Despite these struggles, Fannie Lou did not stop her work to end segregation and help black people register to vote.

HAMER SPEAKS UP

n May 1963, Hamer was still working for SNCC. She and her coworkers helped their black neighbors register to vote. They first taught their neighbors how to read. Then they gave them voter registration practice tests. They talked to them about their rights and responsibilities as US citizens. They also handed out food and clothing donations to poor people.

As part of her job, Hamer was chosen to go to a training program in South Carolina. On the way home, the bus stopped in Winona, Mississippi. Five of Hamer's coworkers entered

Hamer, *middle*, and activists Annie Devine, *left*, and Victoria Gray, *right*, advocated for black people's representation in government.

SUFFRAGE TIMELINE

1870
The Fifteenth Amendment
was ratified.
It gave African American
men the right to vote.

1920
The Nineteenth Amendment
was ratified.
It gave women
the right to vote.

1965
President Lyndon B. Johnson
signed the Voting Rights Act.
This act outlawed
voter discrimination.

Late 1800s
Southern states created obstacles
that kept black people
from registering to vote.
These obstacles included poll taxes
and literacy tests.

1964
The Twenty-Fourth Amendment
was ratified.
It outlawed poll taxes.

The above timeline shows important events related to African Americans' right to vote. Does this timeline help you better understand the obstacles they had to overcome? In what ways did the struggles for women's suffrage and black suffrage overlap?

the bus station. They sat down at a lunch counter to order food. The US Supreme Court had made segregated rest stops illegal. But their white waitress refused to serve them. Hamer got off the bus to see what was going on. Police came and arrested Hamer and her coworkers.

In jail, the police forced two black prisoners to beat Hamer and her coworkers with clubs. The men injured Hamer's kidneys, her leg, and one of her eyes.

The police did not give her medical care. Hamer would suffer from these injuries for the rest of her life.

The police kept Hamer in jail for three days. When they finally released her, she learned some upsetting news. A white man had shot and killed black civil rights leader Medgar Evers.

A NEW DEMOCRATIC PARTY

Evers's death and Hamer's experience in jail inspired her to work even harder to achieve equal rights. She traveled around the United States. She talked at SNCC meetings around

MEDGAR EVERS

Medgar Evers was an African American civil rights activist from Mississippi. He had fought in World War II (1939–1945). He worked with the National Association for the Advancement of Colored People (NAACP). The NAACP helped black people register to vote. The group also fought for equal rights in the workplace. On June 12, 1963, a white man named Byron De La Beckwith shot and killed Evers. Beckwith supported racial segregation. He did not want African Americans to have equal rights.

the country. She told people what had happened to her in Indianola and Winona. Many people were moved by her story.

In June 1963, some African Americans tried to vote in Mississippi's primary election. In primary elections, people vote to nominate candidates for a later election. But Democratic officials did not allow African Americans to vote. White people controlled the Mississippi Democratic Party.

In 1964 Hamer helped found the Mississippi Freedom Democratic Party (MFDP). The MFDP gave black people an alternative to the Mississippi Democratic Party. Hamer and 67 other MFDP members went to the Democratic National Convention (DNC) in Atlantic City, New Jersey. Hamer spoke to the people at the meeting. She described the discrimination black people faced in the South. She asked for change. The MFDP wanted to have delegates at the convention. Delegates vote for the person they want to run for

Hamer, *left*, and MFDP members Victoria Gray, *middle*, and Annie Devine, *right*, read a letter granting them permission to sit in on a political debate in Congress in 1965.

US president. MFDP delegates would give black people representation in the Democratic Party.

PRESIDENT LYNDON B. JOHNSON

President Lyndon B. Johnson was running for reelection in 1964. He saw that Hamer's speeches were getting a lot of attention. He was concerned that the MFDP was trying to take delegates away from the Mississippi Democratic Party. He knew he could count on the delegates from that party to vote for him. He was not sure whether the MFDP would support him. He also worried that Hamer might make him look bad by drawing attention to the Democratic Party's unfair treatment of black voters. For all these reasons, Johnson did not want voters to hear Hamer's DNC speech.

PERSPECTIVES

SPEAKING PLAINLY

Today, many people continue to recognize Hamer for her passion and her iconic speeches. Funmilola Fagbamila is a Nigerian American artist. She said, "Specifically what inspires me about Fannie Lou Hamer is her willingness to . . . address her experience and . . . to not sugarcoat it, to not make it too dense, to say it in a way that everybody can hear it plainly."

Johnson made a last-minute news announcement. He hoped that since he was president, his announcement would be put on the evening news instead of Hamer's speech. But he did not expect what happened after that. Reporters were so impressed with Hamer's speech that they taped it. Her speech aired on the national news after the president's speech.

STRAIGHT TO THE
SOURCE

In Hamer's 1964 DNC speech, she described the threats and violence she and other black people faced:

> *It was the 31st of August in 1962 that eighteen of us traveled twenty-six miles [42 km] to the county courthouse in Indianola to try to register to become first-class citizens. . . . They only allowed two of us in to take the literacy test at the time. After we had taken this test and started back to Ruleville, we was held up . . . [in] Indianola where the bus driver was charged that day with driving a bus the wrong color. . . .*
>
> *Is this America, the land of the free and the home of the brave, where we have to sleep with our telephones off the hooks because our lives be threatened daily, because we want to live as decent human beings?*

Source: Fannie Lou Hamer. "Testimony before the Credentials Committee, Democratic National Convention." *American Public Media.* American Public Media, August 22, 1964. Web. Accessed November 8, 2018.

Consider Your Audience

Adapt this passage for a different audience, such as your friends. Write a blog post conveying this same information for the new audience. How does your post differ from the original text and why?

CHAPTER
FIVE

HAMER'S LEGACY

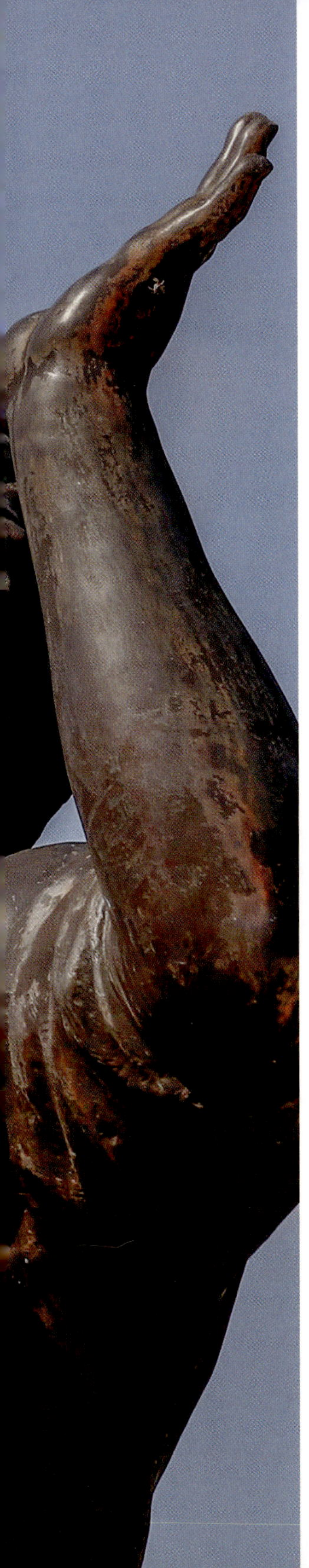

After Hamer's 1964 DNC speech, many people wanted to hear her speak. She traveled throughout the United States. She gave speeches at civil rights meetings. People also came to these meetings to hear Hamer sing. She sang uplifting spiritual and civil rights songs. Hamer's work helped raise money for civil rights organizations.

In early 1964, Hamer attempted to run for a seat in the US Congress. But she was not allowed to put her name on the regular ballot. The MFDP created a special ballot with the names of all the candidates, including Hamer. But this was not considered an official ballot.

A statue of Hamer in Ruleville, Mississippi, honors her life and legacy.

Jamie Whitten won the race instead. Whitten was a white man who had been elected to Congress 12 times before. Still, Hamer's efforts inspired other African Americans to run for office. She set the stage for the MFDP to participate in politics in the future.

HELPING OTHERS

Hamer understood how hard it was to grow up in poverty. She knew that people need food, shelter, and clothing before they can fight for civil rights. She helped gather donations of food and clothes. She gave the donations to poor people in the Mississippi Delta.

Hamer gave a speech at the 1968 Democratic National Convention.

THE 1968 DEMOCRATIC NATIONAL
CHICAGO CONVENTION ILLINOIS

She also helped set up Head Start programs. These programs provide education and health care to children in low-income families.

In July 1964, President Johnson signed the Civil Rights Act. This act ended segregation. It also made it illegal for employers to discriminate against people based on their race or other factors. Then in August 1965, Johnson signed the Voting Rights Act. This act outlawed practices such as literacy tests that kept black people from voting. The efforts of Hamer and other civil rights activists helped bring about these changes.

INSPIRING OTHERS

In 1977 Hamer died of cancer and heart failure. She was 59 years old. Hamer spent her adult life in service to the civil rights movement. She helped black people in the South register to vote. She made more people aware of racial discrimination. She protested police brutality. She helped poor black people in Mississippi make better lives for themselves and their families. She never let fear stop her from fighting for what she believed in. Through her actions, words, and songs, she inspired other people to join in the fight for civil rights.

FAST FACTS

- Fannie Lou Hamer was born in Mississippi on October 6, 1917. She began picking cotton at the age of six and left school to work full time when she was 12 years old.

- In 1944 Fannie Lou married Perry "Pap" Hamer. They worked as sharecroppers in Ruleville, Mississippi. They adopted two girls.

- Hamer attended a meeting of the Student Nonviolent Coordinating Committee (SNCC) in 1962. She found out for the first time that she had the right to vote. She tried to register to vote but could not pass a literacy test.

- Hamer's employer, a plantation owner, fired her for trying to vote. She left the plantation and began to work for SNCC.

- Hamer was arrested while working for SNCC. She was unjustly jailed and badly beaten.

- Hamer helped found the Mississippi Freedom Democratic Party. She spoke at the 1964 Democratic National Convention. President Lyndon B. Johnson tried to stop her speech from being aired on television.

- Hamer died in 1977. Her political work and activism continues to inspire others.

STOP AND
THINK

Tell the Tale

Chapter One of this book discusses Hamer's attempt to register to vote in 1962. Imagine that you live in the South in the 1960s. Write 200 words about the racial discrimination you see. How do white people treat black people? How are black people segregated in public?

Surprise Me

Chapter Two discusses Hamer's childhood and her life as a sharecropper. After reading this book, what two or three facts about the sharecropping system did you find most surprising? Write a few sentences about each fact. Why did you find each fact surprising?

You Are There

This book discusses Hamer's speech at the 1964 Democratic National Convention. Imagine you were in the audience when Hamer gave this speech. Write a letter home telling your friends about your experience. Be sure to add plenty of details to your letter.

GLOSSARY

abolish
to officially end or do away with something

ballot
a ticket or a piece of paper that is used to vote in an election

constitution
the written beliefs and laws of a country

delegate
a person at a convention or conference who represents people in a larger community

discrimination
the unjust treatment of a person or group based on race or other perceived differences

literacy
the ability to read and write

plantation
a large farm where workers grow crops

poverty
the state of being poor

representative
someone chosen to represent a community in the local or federal government

segregation
the separation of people of different races or ethnic groups through separate schools and other public spaces

ONLINE RESOURCES

To learn more about Fannie Lou Hamer, visit our free resource websites below.

Visit **abdocorelibrary.com** or scan this QR code for free Common Core resources for teachers and students, including vetted activities, multimedia, and booklinks, for deeper subject comprehension.

Visit **abdobooklinks.com** or scan this QR code for free additional online weblinks for further learning. These links are routinely monitored and updated to provide the most current information available.

LEARN MORE

Weatherford, Carole Boston. *Voice of Freedom.* Somerville, MA: Candlewick Press, 2015.

Winter, Max. *The Civil Rights Movement.* Minneapolis, MN: Abdo Publishing, 2014.

ABOUT THE
AUTHORS

Duchess Harris, JD, PhD

Dr. Harris is a professor of American Studies at Macalester College and curator of the Duchess Harris Collection of ABDO books. She is also the coauthor of the titles in the collection, which features popular selections such as *Hidden Human Computers: The Black Women of NASA* and series including News Literacy and Being Female in America.

Before working with ABDO, Dr. Harris authored several other books on the topics of race, culture, and American history. She served as an associate editor for *Litigation News*, the American Bar Association Section of Litigation's quarterly flagship publication, and was the first editor in chief of *Law Raza*, an interactive online journal covering race and the law, published at William Mitchell College of Law. She has earned a PhD in American Studies from the University of Minnesota and a JD from William Mitchell College of Law.

Marne Ventura

Marne Ventura has written nearly 80 books for kids. A former elementary school teacher, she holds a master's degree in education from the University of California. Her favorite topics include history, science, arts, crafts, and food. Marne and her husband live in California.

INDEX

American Civil War, 9, 16, 26

childhood, 15–17
Civil Rights Act, 40
Congress, US, 13, 37–38

Democratic National Convention (DNC), 32–34

Evers, Medgar, 31

Fifteenth Amendment, 8, 30
forced sterilization, 19–20

Hamer, Perry "Pap" (husband), 18–19, 25, 27
Head Start programs, 40

Johnson, Lyndon B., 30, 33–34, 40

literacy tests, 7–8, 10, 23, 27, 30, 35, 40

Mississippi Delta, 26, 38
Mississippi Democratic Party, 32–34
Mississippi Freedom Democratic Party (MFDP), 32–33, 37–38

segregation, 10, 20, 27, 30, 31, 40
sharecropping, 15–16, 18, 25, 26
slavery, 9–10, 16, 25, 26
Student Nonviolent Coordinating Committee (SNCC), 20–21, 26–27, 29, 31–32

voting registration, 7–8, 10, 12, 20, 21, 23–24, 27, 29, 30, 31, 35, 40
Voting Rights Act, 30, 40

Whitten, Jamie, 38
women's suffrage, 9, 30